CALL OF THE WILD

The Language of Dolphins and Other Sea Animals

Megan Kopp

Cavendish
Square

New York

Published in 2017 by Cavendish Square Publishing, LLC
243 5th Avenue, Suite 136, New York, NY 10016

Website: cavendishsq.com

This publication represents the opinions and views of the author based on his or her personal experience, knowledge, and research. The information in this book serves as a general guide only. The author and publisher have used their best efforts in preparing this book and disclaim liability rising directly or indirectly from the use and application of this book.

CPSIA Compliance Information: Batch #CS16CSQ

All websites were available and accurate when this book was sent to press.

Library of Congress Cataloging-in-Publication Data

Names: Kopp, Megan, author.
Title: The language of dolphins and other sea animals / Megan Kopp.
Description: New York: Cavendish Square Publishing, [2017] | Series: Call of the wild | Includes bibliographical references and index. | Description based on print version record and CIP data provided by publisher; resource not viewed.
Identifiers: LCCN 2015050993 (print) | LCCN 2015048114 (ebook) | ISBN 9781502617149 (ebook) |
ISBN 9781502617262 (pbk.) | ISBN 9781502617200 (library bound) | ISBN 9781502617088 (6 pack)
Subjects: LCSH: Animal communication—Juvenile literature. | Marine animals—Behavior—Juvenile literature.
Classification: LCC QL776 (print) | LCC QL776 .K67 2017 (ebook) | DDC 591.59—dc23
LC record available at http://lccn.loc.gov/2015050993

Editorial Director: David McNamara
Editor: Kelly Spence
Copy Editor: Rebecca Rohan
Art Director: Jeffrey Talbot
Designer: Joseph Macri
Production Assistant: Karol Szymczuk
Photo Research: J8 Media

Printed in the United States of America

CONTENTS

Animal Communication

Communication is the sharing of information between a sender and a receiver. This information is sent by a **signal**. Signals can be seen, heard, felt, tasted, and smelled. In some cases, signals can be electrical.

SAY WHAT?

Humans speak in words. This is a language other humans understand. Animals have their own ways of sending messages. They communicate in many different ways and for many different reasons.

Male and female sea lions meet on the shore to choose mates.

Some animals communicate to attract a mate. Others use signals to establish control. Communication can be used for defense and to warn about danger. It is also important for teaching young, sharing information about food, showing affection, and playing.

HEY, YOU!

Signals and displays are actions animals use to send information. Sound is often the most common signal used

Sharks rely more on their sense of smell than sight for communication.

by animals. Sound works well because it quickly travels long distances. Other animals can also figure out where the sound came from.

It is important for animals to share locations. Other animals need to know that there is "food that way" or "trouble up ahead." Sound can help animals identify each other. Other types of communication are used to **influence** behavior. "Get out of my space" is a clear command. Stick around and there could be trouble!

Communication is especially important between **social** animals of the same species. Groups of animals need to share information. Humans use words to communicate these messages. Other animals use sound signals such as calls and whistles. Some animals use body language. All are good ways to send a message.

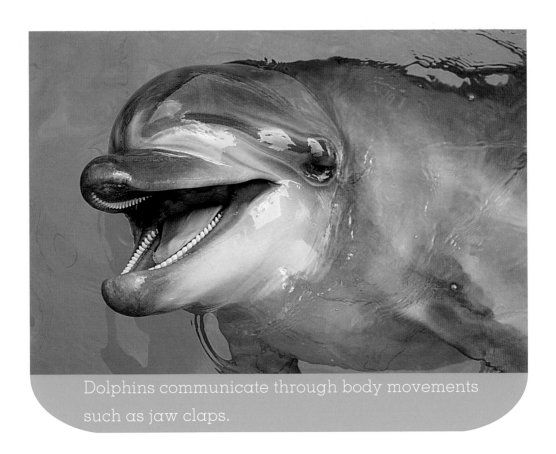

Dolphins communicate through body movements such as jaw claps.

An average pod of dolphins can include anywhere from two to fifteen members.

CHAPTER ONE

Click On Dolphin Chatter

Dolphins communicate using sound, sight, and touch. They do not make sounds with their mouths. Dolphins do not have **vocal cords** like humans do. Instead, a dolphin makes sounds by moving air through its **blowhole**.

Bottlenose dolphins use different whistles to communicate. These include moans, grunts, squeaks, and even creaks. These sounds can be loud or soft. Sometimes they come as a fast series of clicks, called a click train. Click trains show excitement or anger.

Mother dolphins whistle to their calves almost nonstop for several days after their birth. This helps the calves learn to identify their mothers. Baby dolphins have their own unique **signature** whistle by the time they are only one month old.

SPECIES STATS

Bottlenose dolphins are meat eaters. They can grow up to 14 feet (4.3 meters) long and weigh 1,100 pounds (499 kilograms). Bottlenose dolphins live between twenty to forty years in the wild. Groups called **pods** are found in warm, tropical oceans.

SILENT SIGNALS

Dolphins also use other sound signals. They slap the surface of the water with their tails and flippers and clap their jaws. These actions show displeasure. Blowing a stream of bubbles gets the attention of other dolphins. To show **submission**, dolphins look away, flinch, or swim off. They also use touch to communicate by rubbing fins with one other.

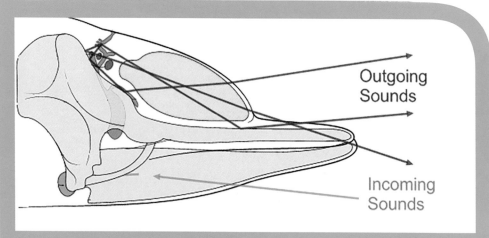

Outgoing Sounds

Incoming Sounds

THE SCIENCE BEHIND ECHOLOCATION

To find food, dolphins send out a series of fast clicks. These sounds travel underwater. When they hit an object, an echo bounces back to the dolphin. This is called **echolocation**. It allows the dolphin to see the world through sound.

Huge groups of sea lions come together on seaside rocks during mating season.

CHAPTER TWO

Sea Lion Speak

Sea lions are one of the most vocal mammals in the world. Like humans, sea lions use their vocal cords to communicate. They bark, growl, and grunt. Sea lions make sounds both above and below the water.

BARK, BARK, AND BARK SOME MORE!

Male sea lions bark nonstop during mating season. This helps them set up and establish their **territory**. Once their territory is defined, they only bark to defend it from other

Two sea lions face off using their powerful voices and body language.

males. Males will also use body movements to signal to other males to back off.

MOM? WHERE ARE YOU, MOM?

There can be thousands of sea lions in a **rookery**. Females use a special call to communicate with their pups. When a mother returns to the rookery after feeding, she needs to find her pup. Both mom and pup call back and forth to locate each other. They also recognize each other by sight and smell.

Female sea lions use sound signals to warn other sea lions to stay away and to warn of danger. These sounds range from squeals to growls. Pups calls to their moms in bleats like

A sea lion pup will stay with its mother for up to one year.

lambs. They also have high-pitched alarm calls. As they grow, young sea lions develop a deeper bark.

SPECIES STATS

Sea lions are meat eaters. There are six species of sea lion. These animals live in groups called a colony or rookery. California sea lions grow up to 7 feet (2.1 m) long and weigh 610 to 860 pounds (277 to 390 kg). They are found along the coast of western North America and near the Galápagos Islands. Few sea lions live beyond thirty years in the wild.

Humpback whales are strong swimmers. They use their powerful tails to move through the water.

CHAPTER THREE

A Whale of a Song

Humpback whales are known for their magical songs. These signals include moans, howls, cries, and other noises. These sounds travel long distances and can last for hours.

BEYOND SONG

Most of the sounds made by humpback whales are not songs. They make a variety of deep and loud sounds. These include moans, grunts, thumps, and knocks. It is believed that these sounds are used to greet and locate other whales, find a mate, **navigate**, and identify one another.

A pod of humpbacks will work together to feed. Some blow bubbles and others make noises to trap a school of fish near the surface of the water.

A TOUCHY SUBJECT

Most male humpback whales are loners. Mothers and their young are often found together. They use touch to communicate. They swim close together, often touching one another with their flippers. This gesture is likely a way to show affection.

SENDING A MESSAGE LOUD AND CLEAR

A humpback lifts its tail out of the water before taking a deep dive.

Some of the sounds a humpback whale makes come from slapping its flippers or tail or by forcing spouts of water through its blowhole. These are body displays. These sounds may be used to show excitement or anger.

SPECIES STATS

Humpback whales eat both plants and animals. Humpback whales are giant animals reaching over 62 feet (19 m) in length. They weigh up to 40 tons (36 metric tons). Groups of humpbacks are called pods. Humpbacks are found in all the world's oceans. Each winter they **migrate** from warm breeding grounds to cooler waters to feed.

STUDYING THE HUMPBACK'S SONG

It is believed that humpbacks sing to attract a partner. Humpback males sing mainly during breeding season. Researchers have recorded humpback whale songs from both sides of the southern Indian Ocean. They discovered that whales living off the coast of Madagascar sing different songs than those living off the coast of Western Australia. Scientists continue to study these sounds to try and understand their meaning.

Great white sharks have an excellent sense of smell. They can sense blood in water up to 3 miles (5 kilometers) away.

Electrifying Shark Encounters

How do sharks communicate with one another? No one knows for sure! Not a lot is known about shark communication. These animals are typically loners. Researchers have not had many chances to study sharks sharing information with each other.

MAKING THE MOVES

Scientists have discovered that great white sharks sometimes swim alongside one another. They open their jaws, move their fins in a certain way, and even have water fights.

A smaller shark will often swim away if a larger shark is nearby.

These actions are some form of communication. Nobody yet knows what they mean. Sharks often gather to feed on large **prey**. In these cases, smaller sharks let larger sharks eat first. Sharks of the same size use slight body movements to settle the question of who is top shark.

SPECIES STATS

Great white sharks are meat eaters. Their prey includes sea lions, seals, small whales, and sea turtles. They range from 15 to more than 20 feet (4.6 to 6 m) in length and weigh up to 5,000 pounds (2,268 kg). Groups of great whites are called schools or shoals. Great white sharks are found mostly along the coasts of Australia, South Africa, California, and the northeastern United States. They live up to thirty years in the wild.

THE SCIENCE BEHIND ELECTRORECEPTION

Sharks have all the usual senses of sight, hearing, taste, touch, and smell. They also have a sixth sense called **electroreception**. Sharks can sense electrical forces from other animals. Only aquatic animals can do this. The shark's nose is filled with special cells. These cells sense the power and direction of the electrical force. Scientists believe this sense is used for navigation and hunting.

Dolphin therapy programs can help children with disabilities, emotional challenges, or other medical issues.

CHAPTER FIVE

A Conversation with Dolphins

Dolphins are found in zoos and aquariums around the world. Some end up there because they were sick or injured and can no longer survive in the wild. Others are born there. Scientists learn a lot about communication by studying these animals.

THE HEALING TOUCH OF A DOLPHIN

Bottlenose dolphins and humans can share special connections. Some programs provide therapy to kids with health issues where they interact with dolphins. The kids learn how to communicate with the dolphins using signals. These experiences can be life-changing.

CONNECTING TO COMMUNICATE

Researchers and trainers work with marine animals in zoos and aquariums to develop a **bond**. Dolphins learn to connect the sound of a whistle with a reward. Rewards include food, toys, or a rub from the trainer. Trainers and researchers also share messages with dolphins by tapping the water and using hand signals.

Dolphins are smart and curious animals that love to explore and play. This Atlantic spotted dolphin is using seaweed as a toy.

IN THE FIELD

Denise Herzing is a scientist who works for the Wild Dolphin Institute. For over twenty-five years, she has been working to learn the language of Atlantic spotted dolphins. Herzing uses a special CHAT (**cetacean** hearing and **telemetry**) box. It sends out dolphin-like whistles. The sounds that the dolphins whistle back are recorded.

Dolphins are smart **mimics**. Herzing trained young dolphins to connect whistle sounds she made up with certain objects. One whistle meant scarf. Another meant rope. The third one was a special whistle for a piece of seaweed used by dolphins as a toy. In 2013, the machine recorded one of the dolphins calling back. It was one of the whistles Herzing had created, meaning seaweed!

Glossary

blowhole The hole on top of a marine mammal's head, such as a dolphin or whale, that is used for breathing.

bond The close connection between two individuals.

cetacean A group of marine mammals including whales and dolphins.

echolocation A process that locates objects using reflected sound.

electroreception The ability of an aquatic animal to distinguish electric fields and currents.

influence To have an effect on someone or something.

migrate To move from one area to another at a particular time of the year.

mimics Individuals that are good at imitating others.

navigate To find your way.

pods Groups of animals, such as whales and dolphins.

prey An animal that is hunted by another animal as food.

rookery A crowded gathering place for sea lions or other animals.

signal A sound or action used to send a message or warning.

signature Something related to a particular individual.

social Living in groups rather than as individuals.

submission Acknowledging the power or dominance of another.

telemetry A method of measuring distance to an object.

territory An area belonging to one individual or group of individuals.

vocal cords Folds in an organ in the throat that vibrate and make sound as air passes over them.

Find Out More

Books

De Silva, Kay. *Dolphins: Amazing Pictures & Fun Facts on Animals in Nature*. Our Amazing World. Camberwell, Australia: CKTY Publishing Solutions, 2015.

Lunis, Natalie. *Humpback Whale: The Singer*. Animal Loudmouths. New York: Bearport Publishing, 2012.

Rizzo, Johnna. *Ocean Animals: Who's Who in the Deep Blue*. Washington, DC: National Geographic Children's Books, 2016.

Websites

National Geographic Kids: Secret Language of Dolphins

kids.nationalgeographic.com/explore/nature/secret-language-of-dolphins/#dolphin-communication.jpg

Read all about these playful animals.

San Diego Zoo: Sea Lions

animals.sandiegozoo.org/animals/sea-lion

Learn fun facts about these animal loudmouths.

Index

About the Author

Megan Kopp is a freelance writer whose passions include science, nature, and the outdoors. She is the author of close to sixty titles for young readers. She loves research and has even gone so far as volunteering to be rescued from a snow cave to get a story about training avalanche rescue dogs. Kopp lives in the foothills of the Canadian Rocky Mountains where she spends her spare time hiking, camping, and canoeing. One of her dreams is to kayak British Columbia's Haida Gwaii and see some of the area's marine life, including sea lions, whales, and orcas.